TRY THIS ONE... STRIKES AGAIN

IDEAS FOR YOUTH GROUPS

Edited by Cindy S. Hansen

Designed by Jean Bruns

Illustrations by Alan Wilkes,
Martin Bucella and Jean Bruns

P.O. Box 481
Loveland, CO 80539

Selected from the regular feature "Try This One"
in GROUP, the youth ministry magazine.

TRY THIS ONE... STRIKES AGAIN

Copyright © 1984 by Thom Schultz Publications, Inc.

Library of Congress Catalog No. 84-81781
ISBN 0931-529-00-X

All rights reserved. No part of this book may be reproduced in any manner whatsoever without written permission from the publisher, except in the case of brief quotations embodied in critical articles and reviews. For information write Permissions, Group Books, P.O. Box 481, Loveland, CO 80539.

CONTENTS

Introduction 4
Fun 'n Games 5
Special Occasions 31
Group Growth Goodies 47
Fun Fund Raisers 63
Note 79

INTRODUCTION

Why are new ideas hard to think of when you need them the most? To help meet the never-ending need for new activities, GROUP Magazine created the "Try This One" section. In "Try This One," youth group members and leaders from across the country submit successful and original activities that work in their groups.

Try This One ... Strikes Again is the fourth compilation of activities for crowdbreakers, games, special occasions, group growth ideas and fund raisers.

Use this gold mine of activities to:
- add spice to your meetings
- entertain during a family fun night
- get the youth mingling during a retreat
- create a new worship setting
- raise money for projects and trips

Feel free to adapt, add to or combine ideas to make them suitable for your group's needs. Then create new, original ideas of your own and send them to us. See the note on page 79 for more details.

FUN 'N GAMES

BACK ART

This game could lead into a discussion on communication or gossip. Have your group form teams of six people. Instruct each team to sit in a line, one person behind another, and take a vow of silence for the duration of the game. Give the first person in each line a pencil and a piece of paper. Then show the last person in each line a simple hand-drawn picture of an object (a house, cat, car). That person must use his or her finger to draw the object on the back of the person in front of him or her, and so on. When the drawing reaches the first person in line, he or she must draw it on the piece of paper. Have judges determine which team's picture most resembles its original picture. If time permits, play more rounds, letting team members change positions if they want.

—Kathie Taylor, Stamford, Connecticut

BOUNCING BALL DISCUSSION

Try this one when a discussion appears ready to bite the dust. Bounce a red rubber ball back and forth to group members. The person who catches the ball must add a comment to the discussion. (Limit on speaking time: one minute.) Then the speaker bounces the ball to another member, who adds a comment. Bouncing the ball to the shyer members helps encourage response.

Our discussions seem more lively and stimulating whenever that ball starts bouncing.
—Waneen Tulloch, Belton, Texas

BUBBLE FUN

For full-blown fun and an activity bubbling with possibilities, concoct your own bubble solution: one tablespoon dish detergent, two tablespoons water and four drops of corn syrup. Create giant bubbles by adding glycerine and a pinch of sugar. (Glycerine is inexpensive and available at drugstores.) Provide a rainbow of mixtures by simply adding food coloring.

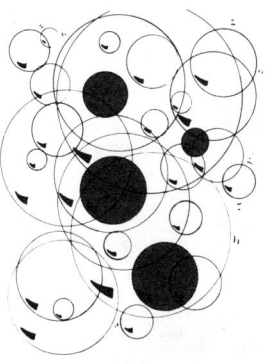

Raid the kitchen, office and other unlikely places for blower utensils. Try your hand at blowing and breezing through whisks, sieves, slotted spoons, bent paper clips, scissor handles, wire, coat hangers or plastic six-pack holders.

Hold a contest. Then blow it! Award bubble gum prizes to the most "pop"ular in each category. Competition could include the biggest, oddest, zaniest or most colorful bubble. Join efforts and create a giant group bubble sculpture.

Your bubble mix could provide not only fun, but funds! Collect bottles and jars, design a bubble-label and sell your special bubble mix.

BUBBLE GUM CROWDBREAKER

Having trouble finding new ways to break your group into small groups? Try this one.

As your kids arrive, selectively distribute different-colored bubble gum and ask them to chew only the gum you've provided. If you want three small groups, hand out three colors; if you want four small groups, hand out four colors; etc.

To split into the groups, ask kids to blow bubbles and get together with other kids who have the same-colored bubbles.

If you later want to further divide the groups, have a bubble-blowing contest. Pass out more gum to group members who have discarded their original wads (colors don't matter at this point). Choose the three kids who blow the largest bubbles to form a group; choose the three kids whose bubbles pop first to form another group; and continue this process until everyone belongs to a new small group.

—David Washburn, Brockport, New York

COME-AS-YOU-WERE PARTY

Bring out the best in your group! Have a "Come-as-You-Were Party"—it may be a highlight of the year.

Inconspicuously collect photos of your youth group members in a variety of situations. Get one photo of each person in your group in something such as a sports uniform, cheerleading outfit, play costume, tutu, suit and tie, formal, grubbies, swimsuit, winter coat or shorts. Plan to attend events where the youth will be dressed such ways or ask parents to provide photos. Be creative.

When you have a photo of each youth group member dressed in an unusual way, post the photos on the church bulletin board and advertise a "Come-as-You-Were Party." To get in, the youth must be dressed as they were in the photos. Invite a photographer to take a group photo—it will make a great poster.

—Tommy Baker, Florence, Kentucky

COUNTRY BANQUET

We used this banquet to honor our youth workers and give information about upcoming events.

Invitations asked guests to dress "country" (overalls, checkered shirts, straw hats). We decorated the banquet hall with kerosene lamps, quilts, baskets of apples and potatoes, farm-fresh "aigs," cans of fruit and vegetables, calico stuffed chickens and mountain dew jugs.

As the guests arrived, they received a packet including sheets of youth news and plans, a bandanna, a clothespin name tag and a knock-knock joke with a number on it.

During the country-style meal, we called out numbers of the knock-knock jokes; the persons with those jokes had to stand and read them to an eager audience.

Following the informational "program" part of the gathering, we had "volunteers" star in a country-theme melodrama which was created especially for the banquet.

We then challenged small groups to create the longest list of uses for a bandanna. This was a riot.

Plenty of country songs, a short devotion and "Amazing Grace" with a harmonica solo in the middle ended our country banquet.

—Gwyn Baker, Knoxville, Tennessee

COW CRAZY

Our youth group had a great time at a five-hour "Cow Crazy" event at a farm. Yours can, too—here's how.

Go to a farm for an afternoon and early evening, play "cow games" and have a cookout. Here are some games we used:

Mooing contest. Let group members practice first, then moo one at a time for your judge—the farmer. The most realistic moo wins.

Feed the baby cow. Split your group into two teams for this relay. Team members run one at a time to a table holding small baby bottles and each drinks all the juice from a bottle.

Milk the cow. Again, two teams and a relay. Each team member races to fill a cup with milk from a gentle cow. (This game is best if preceded by a milking demonstration.)

Corral the cows. In a big field, two group members are "it." They join hands and run around trying to tag others, who then must also join hands and help tag people. The last "cow" to be "corralled" wins.

Cow chip search and toss. First, a search for the biggest chip. Then, the toss: The person who throws a chip the farthest wins.

After our cookout we gathered in the barn for singing and a brief message from the youth pastor.

A hayride topped off our successful "Cow Crazy."

—Sylvia Carlson, Dallas, Texas

DRAGON DODGE BALL

Separate your group into teams of four people. Then choose one team to be the first dragon; have the kids line up and put their hands on the waist of the person in front of them. Instruct the other teams to join together and form a large circle around the dragon. Give a ball to the players in the circle; they need to throw the ball at the last person of the dragon and hit him or her below the waist. When hit, he or she joins the circle and the players try to hit the (new) last person of the dragon. This continues until only one person of the dragon is left and he or she, too, is hit. Then the next team of four forms a new dragon that must dodge the ball. Be sure to time the life span of each dragon; the team whose dragon survives the longest is the winner.

—Kathie Taylor, Stamford, Connecticut

FEED THE ARK RELAY

Noah's ark inspired us to develop this icebreaker. We made two head masks that looked like arks. Well, sort of. Nothing fancy. They can be created from posterboard, construction paper or whatever. Each ark had a door that opened to the wearer's mouth.

We then split into two teams. One person from each team donned the ark and sat on the floor across the room. The other teammates lined up single file at the other end of the room. Each was given a spoon and an animal cracker. At "GO!" the first racer (animal cracker in spoon; spoon handle in mouth) hurried to the ark. At the ark, the racer pulled the boat's door open and spoon-fed the animal cracker to the person inside. If the relay racer dropped the cracker, a new one had to be obtained back at the starting line. The teams' objective was to feed all the animals to the ark.

If you want to get fancy, a few folks with squirt guns can "rain" on the racers.

—Edward D. Uhles, Kirkland, Washington

FIVE-MINUTE WORSHIP

Here's a discussion starter for the topic of worship.

Divide group members into small group "congregations." Give each young person a card with a description of a person he or she must represent. The small groups each have five minutes to plan a worship service that will include "something for everyone."

Suggestions of people for your group members to represent: rock 'n roll musician; 85-year-old widow; someone who only goes to church on Easter and Christmas; opera

12

singer; computer expert; 5-year-old hyperactive boy; deaf mother; 17-year-old girl who is forced to attend church; farmer who is at his first church service; 30-year-old single parent.

When the five minutes are up, let the small groups present their worship services to the entire group.

This exercise is both hilarious and a good lead into a Bible study on worship or a planning session for a real worship service.

—Bryan Blomker, Eden Valley, Minnesota

FUTURE FANTASTIC

Start the new year with a bang! Hold a "Future Fantastic" meeting with your group.

Members should come dressed as people of the future—or you can provide zany "dress" items.

Have your young people help decorate the meeting area to look as if it's in a future time. Provide futuristic background music.

Award prizes for best costumes.

Now, creatively tell or "tease" your group members about upcoming events. You might show them items that relate to or suggest the activities in some way. Let group members suggest what things they'd like the group to do in the "future."

Discuss topics that will concern group members when they're adults.

If you have time, show an outer space or "future" film.

Serve out-of-this-century refreshments (have creative group members "alter" food to look like what we'll eat in the future.)

—Steve Allen, Ironton, Ohio

GLUG

All you need for "Glug" are two to six gallons of Kool-Aid, a straw for each member and two equal containers. It's best to play "Glug" outside.

It's a simple game. Divide into two equal teams. Each member dips a straw into the Kool-Aid-filled container. The first team to finish off its container wins.

"Glug" is fun, hilarious, simple, easy, dreadful (if you ever do it again), fulfilling, and mighty gross when Kool-Aid-flavored air bubbles begin re-entry by means of burping contests afterward.

—Lennie Spooner, Lewiston, Idaho

GROUP NOISE CONTEST

The "Group Noise Contest" is a fun way to start a meeting. Divide into groups of equal size. The size of the groups can range from three to 10 members. Each group is given a cassette tape recorder, a blank tape and a sheet of instructions. Dismiss the groups to different rooms.

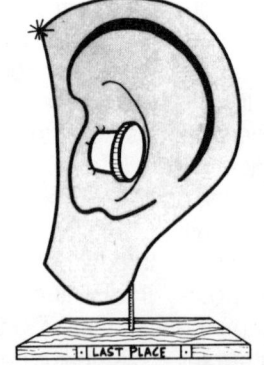

Once in the rooms, each group reads the instruction sheet: "Your group has 15 minutes to record the sounds listed below. The sounds must last at least 10 seconds but no more than 15

seconds. All members of the group must contribute."

A few noise suggestions: herd of restless cows, cat in a dog pound, television show theme song, love-sick coyotes on a moonlit night, sounds of an accident, common hymn.

After 15 minutes, the groups come back together. One at a time, the groups play their first sound. Once all groups have played the first sound, they play the second, then the third, and so on. An "impartial" judge picks the winning group for each noise.

—Gary Hunziker, Chehalis, Washington

HAT ROLES

Here's a role play with a twist: Everyone knows your role—except you.

Before the event, make circle "hats." Write different traits and expected reactions on 18-inch strips of construction paper. Examples are: "Expert: Ask my opinion," "Comedian: Laugh at me," "Helpless: Help me," "Important: Listen to me," and "Stupid: Ignore me." Think of others.

Staple or tape each strip at the ends to make a circle.

Place the hats on your kids' heads without letting anyone read what his or her hat says. Then proceed with a group discussion—about the economy, news item or whatever. Everyone should act toward others according to the instructions on the hats.

After about 15 minutes, end the discussion and have group members try to guess what their hats say. This can lead to reflections on how your youth feel when they're treated certain ways and whether they tend to play the roles in life that others seem to expect of them.

—Ann E. Davis, College Place, Washington

ICE CREAM SPECIAL

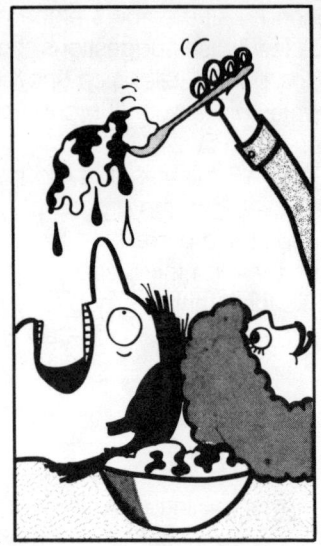

This game is for those of you who love to make and eat ice cream sundaes. Have your kids pair off and create one sundae for each couple. No skimping on those gooey toppings.

Now, the race begins. Have each couple lie on the floor in a straight line on their backs with their heads touching. Place their ice cream sundaes and spoons beside their heads. Each person has to feed the sundae to the person whom his or her head is touching. All heads must remain flat on the floor. The first couple to consume their sundae (with more inside them than on them!) wins the race.

And don't forget to reward your winners with a gift certificate to an ice cream parlor.

—Lance Eisele, Aberdeen, Idaho

INDOOR FLYING SAUCERS

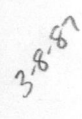

When rain doused our planned "Ultimate Frisbee" game, our group created an indoor version and called it "Indoor Ultimate." The game is played with a foam rubber disc (cut to any size that can be airborne) instead of a Frisbee.

The group divides into two teams. The object of the game is to put the disc into the other team's goal (a 10-foot-by-20-foot area marked with masking tape). Goals are at opposite ends of a room. The disc can be moved only by tossing it. Players may not run with it. Players may run only if they do not possess the disc. If the disc hits the floor, play is stopped. The team that touched it last loses possession to the other team. A goal is scored when a player puts the disc into the other team's goal. The foam disc flies some tricky paths and damages nothing.

Our group loved it. Everyone forgot about the rain outside; we were having an ultimate time indoors.

—Paul Parzik, Largo, Florida

ITCHY FOOT THEATER

This crazy idea takes no talent or acting ability. All you need are teams of kids, a large cardboard box, laundry markers and a number of relatively non-ticklish bare feet. Here's how this toe acting works.

Divide your group into teams of three or four. Then give each team a Bible passage, role, situation or whatever to act out. Unlike most role plays or skits, though, kids' feet are the only things that get into the act.

Each team works out a simple script and decides which feet will be the actors (actresses?). Then they use the laundry markers to make people, animals or objects out of the soles of the feet and toes. If you want to get real fancy, use bits of cloth, paper, cardboard and tape to make tiny arms, legs and outfits. The teams are limited only by their imaginations and craziness.

Cut the back out of the large cardboard box. Cut a hole in the other side of it. Staple a colorful cloth over the inside of the opening and you have an instant stage and curtain.

Have the Athlete's Foot Performers sit on the floor and stick their feet through the curtain.

Bring your camera and take some future movie star's foot shots. Also give a can of foot powder to the team with the best performance.

KING TUT'S RING

Want a fun icebreaker guaranteed to get a bunch of laughs? Then here's a game for you! All you need is a ring and blindfold. Put four or five people in a separate room so they can't see or hear what will happen. Then choose one person to be the honored King Tut. He places the ring on his finger, sits in a chair, then bends low to the floor with that ring finger.

One at a time the people from the other room are blindfolded, brought into the presence of King Tut, and told to bow down and kiss his ring. After they kiss it, King Tut immediately places the ring on one of his toes. Be ready for some yelling and laughing when the blindfold is removed!

—Brenda Haynes, Plummer, Idaho

LAME GAME

Basic games are fun, but sometimes crazy variations are more fun. Variations can include handicapping the players or changing the rules (or both).

Here's a rule-change version of kickball that my junior highers enjoy:

1. Instead of running from first to second to third, you must run from third to second to first, then home.
2. Only fly balls are acceptable; all grounders (kicks below waist level) are out.
3. You do not "get out" when your fly ball is caught.
4. Either play the regular three outs per side or set a

time limit with no restriction on outs.

It takes the kids a while to get used to running the bases backward and remember that when a fly ball is caught the kicker isn't out. This is a good lame game both to play and watch. Why not invite parents for fun? For still more fun apply these lame rules to other base games (e.g., softball and baseball).

—Kevin Jones, Santa Ana, California

LEADER'S NIGHT OFF

Here's a great way to increase group members' participation in a meeting and give the leader a "breather" from his or her normal role.

Before the meeting, the leader writes instructions on individual slips of paper for various segments of the meeting such as "choose and lead songs," "open in prayer," "choose a Bible passage and read it to the group," "offer a few thoughts on getting along with parents."

The leader passes these slips of paper to members as they arrive at the meeting. Allow a few moments for organizing thoughts and the meeting's order. Then, start the session.

As a youth leader, I've been very pleased with how well and quickly our group always comes up with fresh and creative ideas.

—John Stumbo, Monticello, Minnesota

LIAR'S LINES

This is a good "bluffer's" game. Each person in the group writes answers to four questions. Three of the answers are to be true and one is to be a lie. Some suggested questions: What is the farthest place you've been from home? What is the dumbest thing you've ever done? What was something you were told not to do as a child but did it anyway? What is your favorite song?

Each person reads his or her answers to the group. The others guess which one is the lie. After all have guessed, the person tells which answer was the lie.

This activity always gets a few laughs and also helps group members get to know each other a little more.

—Glenn Davis, Winston-Salem, North Carolina

MIRROR MESSAGES

How can you get publicity mailings to reflect that an event will be fun?

Here's one way that's worked with our group.

Draw a funny-looking face on a piece of paper and cut eye holes. On the other side, write your greeting and introductory message, instructing the readers to look through the eye holes at a mirror to get the rest of the message.

On the funny-face side, carefully write your important event news **backward**.

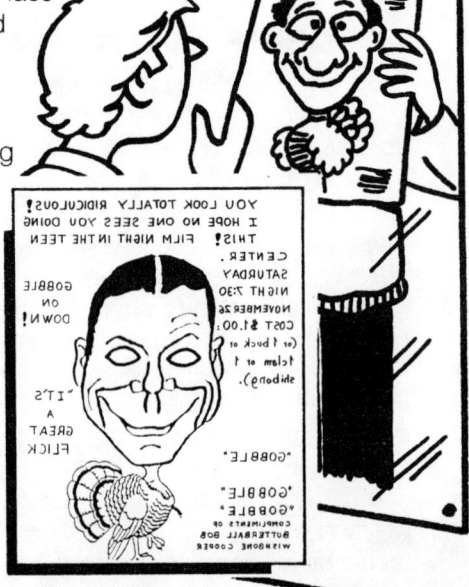

Your group members are sure to get a laugh—and to read the event publicity information.

—Richard Cooper, Memphis, Tennessee

MUSICAL CLOTHES GRAB

This fun activity is an adaptation of "Musical Chairs." Form a circle and play music. While the music plays, pass a bag of clothes around the circle. Whenever the music stops, the person holding the bag must immediately reach into the bag, pull out a piece of clothing and wear it for the rest of the session.

Load the bag with things such as old shower caps, baggy jeans, grimy T-shirts and hole-infested socks. Our group has had really fun times playing this game.

—Lani Ryan, West Monroe, New York

MUSICAL TRUST WALK

This variation of the familiar trust walk will keep your group members on their toes.

Choose a variety of instruments or sounds to indicate signals and directions. For example, a drum could mean "stop"; cymbals could mean "turn right"; wood blocks banged together could mean "turn left"; a whistle could mean "go up or down steps." Match group members with the sounds; one person will be the "left turn" person, another the "stop" person, etc.

Allow time for your sound people to practice and for the other group members to familiarize themselves with the sounds and the related meanings.

Now take your first volunteer from the room. Have everyone else help to quickly set up a maze or obstacle course by moving furniture and/or lying on the floor. Determine the ending point of the maze and make sure your sound people are ready.

Blindfold the person who was taken from the room and bring him or her back. The sound people must cooperate to send him or her through the maze. Remind sound people that the direction the person will go depends on which way he or she is facing when the sound is given.

You may want to change sound people, have different people go through the maze or alter the maze.

Use this activity as an introduction to a discussion on cooperation.

—Carmen Linda Conklin and
Wanda L. Orric, Nashua, Iowa

NAME GAME

Do your group members know what their names really mean? Lead them in this discovery and understanding of the spiritual meanings of their names. You'll need a book of literal meanings of (first) names (some supermarkets and most bookstores have these); Bibles; and enough concordances for each person to have access to one.

Provide each member with a large sheet of colored construction paper and colored markers. Demonstrate how to draw a shield with four sections. Have each group member write his or her first name (no nicknames) in the top section of the shield.

Now read aloud, for all to hear, the literal meaning of each name, which each respective group member will write in the second section of his or her shield. If a name isn't in your book, a quick call to the

STEPHEN

CROWN or GARLAND
-GREEK-

"HENCE FORTH THERE IS LAID UP FOR ME A CROWN OF RIGHTEOUSNESS, WHICH THE LORD, THE RIGHTEOUS JUDGE, SHALL GIVE ME AT THAT DAY: AND NOT TO ME ONLY, BUT UNTO ALL THEM ALSO THAT LOVE HIS APPEARING."
2 TIMOTHY 4:8

I AM TO HELP OTHERS RECEIVE THEIR AWAITING CROWN.

parents may provide the literal meaning.

Each group member now uses a Bible and concordance to find a Bible verse that conceptualizes the literal meaning of his or her name. Help group members think of alternate words if their literal-meaning words aren't listed in the concordance.

Have group members write in the third section of their shields the verses they find. And in the last section, they should write related spiritual meanings they can apply to their lives.

Close this activity by having each member show his or her shield to the group.

—Steve Newton, Sunnyvale, California

NEW LIFE FOR OLD FILMSTRIPS

For fun with films, here's an activity your group will love. You may even discover previously hidden talent.

Collect your church's old filmstrips. Try to find a variety such as Bible stories, cartoons, different settings and situations.

Pass out the filmstrips along with cassette recorders and blank cassette tapes to groups of five or six. Challenge them to look at the strips, write new scripts and tape them (complete with the "beeps"). Let the kids choose whether their products will be humorous or serious or some of each.

Allow 30 minutes for the groups to create their scripts. Then provide plenty of popcorn and get everyone together for the presentation.

The results will be better than going to a double feature at the drive-in.

—Kenn Hines, Concord, Georgia

NEW TWIST TO AN OLD SONG

An old song in new "wineskins" turned out to be a good crowdbreaker for one of our retreats. Basically, the idea is to put a new twist to a familiar song.

Almost everyone is familiar with the song "Hallelu, Hallelu," with the lyrics, "Hallelu, hallelu, hallelu, hallelu-jah; Praise ye the Lord." (**Songs,** compiled by Yohann Anderson, Songs and Creation, Inc., P.O. Box 7, San Anselmo, Calif., 94960). It is usually done with guys standing and singing "hallelu" and the girls responding with "praise ye the Lord."

Most of our people, however, were bored by this over-sung song.

So, we had the kids pair off, turn their backs to each other and lock arms. The oldest of each pair faced the song leader. The "hallelu" was assigned to the older person, the "praise ye the Lord" to the younger. The "new twist" came when each singer, arms locked at all times, had to face the song leader when he or she sang. We tried it slowly at first, and then sped it up the second and third time.

The new twist turned boredom into laughter at our retreat. Other "twisted" familiar songs should make excellent crowdbreakers.

—Leigh Bond, Fort Worth, Texas

NOODLE DOODLES

You may discover new talent with this one. Give paper and pencils to the youth group members. Have them set the paper on top of their heads and tell them what to

draw (an object in the room, a person they all know). They should draw the same thing—and don't let them remove the paper from their heads until they're finished. Collect and display the masterpieces; judges should determine which is best, funniest, etc. Award your winners with colored pencils to encourage futher development of their talent.
—Janet Ridall, Holloman Air Force Base, New Mexico

PASS THE CARROT

Have everyone form a circle. Place a carrot between the knees of the tallest person; he or she must pass the carrot to the knees of the person to the left, without using hands. This continues until the carrot has traveled around the circle. Then break off a piece and send it around again. If a person drops the carrot, he or she is out of the game. The last person left is the winner. Give him or her a fresh carrot to take home.
—Janet Ridall, Holloman Air Force Base, New Mexico

PEEL OUT

"Peel Out" is a "citrusy" exercise in cooperation. Form two groups of boy/girl couples. Each couple receives an orange to peel and eat. However, couples may not use either hands or feet.

To begin, each male wedges his orange in his mouth. At "go" the female rips off the peel with her teeth. Couples may pass the orange from mouth to mouth to remove the peel. If the orange falls to the floor, it must be picked up by the teeth. Once peeled, the couples must eat the orange without using hands or feet. The first group of couples to peel and eat the oranges is the winner.

I know this sounds like a messy, crazy game. It is.

—Dennis Henn, Wenatchee, Washington

PICTURE CHARADES

This relay activity draws out some of your members' artistic communication talents. Divide the group into teams of four to six members. Give felt-tip pens and paper to each team.

A representative from each team approaches the game leader. The game leader discreetly shows each representative a slip of paper. The slip has the name of an object written on it, e.g., paper clip, toothpaste tube, doughnut, sailboat, pepperoni pizza, Christmas tree.

The representatives race back to their teams and silently draw the item for the teammates. The first team that calls out the exact name of the item wins the round. Then another representative is chosen and the game repeated. The team with the most correct guesses wins the game.

—Richard B. Hanna, Fort Myers, Florida

PICTURE STORY

This fun game really gets the yarns spinning. Before the meeting, cut out photographs and illustrations from magazines. Paste them on one side of 5x8 cards. At the meeting, the group sits in a circle. Each person receives a card, blank side up. No one is to look at the other side of the card.

One person begins by showing the photograph to the group. He or she then starts the story, inspired by the card. Really ham it up. When the leader says "change," the person stops the story. The person next to the storyteller shows his or her card and then continues the story. Follow the story around the circle, each person altering it to fit his or her card. Award a children's storybook to the best yarn spinner. The story may not be a literary classic, but it sure is hilarious.

—Karen Hartman, Prince George, British Columbia

3-8-87

PINGPONG PLUNGE

Here's one more crazy pingpong ball crowdbreaker for your group to try.

You'll need an 8-foot-high ladder, a plastic cup and five pingpong balls. Set up the ladder in the middle of your meeting area, place the cup on the floor in front of it and line up the balls on top of the ladder.

Split your group into pairs and let the fun begin:

The first pair has one partner kneel facing the ladder and hold the cup in his or her mouth. The other partner must climb the ladder so that his or her face is even with the top of the ladder where the five pingpong balls are lined up. He or she then blows the balls, one at a time, off the ladder and into the cup below. The partner with the cup may freely move about to <u>catch the balls but must remain kneeling and continue holding the cup</u> by the <u>mouth</u>. No hands allowed.

The <u>partners switch positions and repeat</u> the process. Keep score. A pair scores six if they succeed in six of the 10 tries to get the balls in the cup.

1 point when ball goes into cup

Give all the pairs a turn. The winning pair is the one who gets the most balls in. If there's a tie, have your runners-up repeat the process.

—Scott Welch, Nicholasville, Kentucky

ROLLER SKATE SNAKE

Here's an idea to liven up your next roller skating party.

Divide skaters into three teams and ask for a volunteer from each team. Have all other team members form "snakes" by squatting down on their skates and holding onto the skaters in front of them. Give the person at the front of each snake one end of a rope to hold.

Now the competition begins: Each volunteer should skate to his or her team at the sound of your whistle, grab the loose end of the rope, and pull the snake across the rink or a certain distance. The winning team is the one whose snake remains the most intact.

For added fun, invite your pastor, youth counselors or other adults to pull the snakes. Or have a sophomore pull one snake, a junior another and a senior the other.

—Tim Giessler, Bristol, Pennsylvania

THE SAMSON HAIRCUT

Some hairstyles seem to affect a whole culture. Just look at the recent fashion trends. My hair needed a trim, so I decided to use the experience in youth work. Hence, "The Samson Haircut."

Without telling the group what was going on, I spread a tarp on the floor. I then sat on a stool in the middle of the tarp. A hairdresser from our church began cutting my hair as I read about Samson (Judges 13—16). I wore my weightlifting health spa T-shirt for extra effect.

The result was a fun way to share a Bible story. I think our kids will remember Samson, especially at haircut time.

—Tom Franks, Hayward, California

SEARCH AND SCROUNGE SMORGASBORD

Our youth group held a "Search and Scrounge Smorgasbord" and had a great time preparing a banquet fit for a king.

Here's how it works: (1) Advertise it as an "S and S Smorgasbord." Don't let members know that it stands for "Search and Scrounge Smorgasbord" until they arrive at the event. (2) Each person pays $1 (or any amount you choose). (3) The group is divided into five teams and chooses (out of a hat) one course of five elements to a meal—appetizer, salad, main dish, dessert and beverage. (4) Each team is given an equal amount of money and has two hours in which to go out and search, scrounge, barter or buy the necessary ingredients to prepare and deliver its part of the meal. (The teams may not spend more than they were given.)
(5) When they return two hours later, have a feast. Awards can be given for: most creativity, flavor, quantity, best use of money, etc. Appropriate prizes can then be awarded.

As an example of creativity, one of our teams returned with a large platter of pancakes . . . with 31 different flavors. Another team prepared two large pots of fantastic homemade vegetable soup. A great event!

—Greg Chantler, Tacoma, Washington

SPECIAL OCCASIONS

THE NEW ME

New Year's offers a convenient opportunity to see where we have been and where Christ's unlimited power to change us may lead. "The New Me" is a learning experience that celebrates God's work through us and sets goals for his work in us for the coming year.

The materials needed for the experience include a piece of posterboard (at least 14 inches by 17 inches), sheets of paper, writing utensils, creative materials (cotton balls, construction paper, markers, toothpicks, etc.), the Bible and glue. You'll also need an instant-developing camera and film (or photos of each member brought from home).

Photograph each person as he or she arrives. Pass out the paper and writing utensils. Instruct the members to: List up to 10 good changes you've seen in yourself within the last year. Then list up to 10 concerns or problems you're struggling with. Share these lists in pairs or trios. Then read 2 Corinthians 5:17 and Colossians 3:1-4. Discuss briefly how you've seen Christ change people.

Write 10 goals for yourself for the coming year. Narrow this to the five most realistic ones. Write your five goals and the biblical passages onto your piece of posterboard. Then paste your photo somewhere on the poster.

Now, go from poster to poster, reading everyone's five goals. On each person's poster, write one or two things that you appreciate about him or her. Finally, return to your own poster and embellish it with the creative materials. Take your poster home, tack it on your bedroom wall and read it occasionally as you change and grow through Christ this coming year.

FRACTURED VALENTINES

Our group had a lot of fun with a "Fractured Valentine's" Day party.

Each person receives a hilariously disjointed message.

Before the party, design a crazy-looking valentine,

listing four parts to the message: (Be sure to leave plenty of space between the lines. You'll want to experiment with different valentine designs and choose the one that works best.)

1. Dear _____
2. I want you to be my valentine because _____
3. The thing I like most about you is _____
4. Love, _____

Photocopy a number of these valentine messages.

At the party, hand out the blank valentines and instruct everyone to write his or her name in blank 1. Then fold and tape the top over his or her name. It is important that no one sees the names. Valentines are then gathered and randomly redistributed. Everyone fills in blank 2 with a funny message. Fold down the top to cover blank 2. Gather and redistribute again. Everyone then fills in blank 3 and signs his or her name in blank 4. Gather all valentines.

The youth leader reads the valentines aloud to the group. Be alert to edit any portions of the valentine which might be embarrassing to the receiver.

—Andy Robertson, Hueytown, Alabama

OUTDOOR EASTER DECORATIONS

It's not uncommon to decorate outdoors during the Christmas season—so why not do the same for Easter?

Have youth group members decide how to decorate. Will you use balloons, banners, posters, streamers, ribbon, kites, giant butterflies, windsocks, giant kiosks? Collect, construct or buy the decorations. Some stores, businesses and individuals may be happy to donate or loan certain items. Ask your church boards to donate some money to help with costs. It's okay to make an investment because you can use the decorations from year to year.

Recruit a few extra-early birds on Easter morning to put up all the decorations before the first church service. That usually means **before** sunrise. Attach your decorations to tree limbs, light poles, church steps, railings or the church itself. Create a celebration of color, movement and new life!

And here's a way to involve the entire congregation in the act: Make and distribute Easter "kits." Fill lunch sacks with decoration "ingredients"—balloons, assorted crepe paper streamers, string, a butterfly pattern. Include suggestions and instructions such as a banner idea, new-life Bible verses or an explanation of different Easter symbols. Suggest that planning and decorating be a family project. Ask all church families to display their decorations outside their homes on Easter morning.

This artistic activity can be a powerful witness to the entire community. It says that the church and the Resurrection victory are not just on the corner of Sixth and Vine—but everywhere God's people live!

—Trinity Lutheran Church, Hudson, Wisconsin

SUPERMINUTE

Your group can design one of the most powerful and touching minutes of your church's Easter service. Have interested kids in your group interview on cassette tape people in the church and community answering the questions: "What does Easter mean to you?" and "Describe an Easter that you remember as being really meaningful or happy to you." Be sure to interview small children as well as adults.

Play the cassettes back to your group and choose the best remarks. Be sure to keep track of which comments are on what cassettes. Use recorders with counters if you have them. Next, arrange the comments in a logical or interesting sequence.

Then use another cassette player and blank cassette to record the various comments in the order you want them.

On Easter play the cassette for the rest of the church, using the church's sound system.

Use the "Superminute" concept for other occasions or celebrations. (For instance, on Mother's Day record little kids describing their mommies.)

SINGING MOM-O-GRAMS

Organize a Mother's Day corsage and singing-card delivery service! Here's how:

Three weeks before Mother's Day, advertise your services with a special insert in your church bulletin or newsletter, hang posters, etc. We offered either the silk-flower corsage or the mom-o-gram, or both at a "sale" price. Charge about $5 for single services and $8 for both, depending on your estimate of the cost of the materials.

Two weeks before, take orders and collect as much of the money as possible. Purchase the silk flowers, ribbons, pins (for the corsages) and card-making supplies.

Then one week ahead of time, get everyone together to make the corsages and cards—and practice singing. The tune to "We Wish You a Merry Christmas" adapts well. If you choose to send delivery persons out in pairs, find the best voice combinations.

Deliver the mom-o-grams and corsages on the day before Mother's Day so all the proud moms can wear their corsages on the big day.

Our group had great fun providing this service for our church last year—and we made a profit of $150.

—Richard W. Ferris, Jamestown, North Dakota

HOW WAS YOUR SUMMER?

A great beginning-of-the-school-year game is "How Was Your Summer?" The answers will get some great laughs.

Everyone is given four slips of paper. Each person recalls one unusual thing that happened to him or her during the summer. Mark the four slips with one of these questions: Who? Where? What were you wearing? What were you doing? Now, keeping the unusual summer memory in mind, answer the four questions. For example: Who? "Bill." Where? "Was in Texas." What were you wearing? "Wearing cowboy clothes." What were you doing? "The horse I was riding bucked me off onto a big cowchip." Keep it brief.

Collect the slips into four containers keeping all the "Who?" responses together, "Where?" together, and so on. Then each person draws one slip out of each container. One person at a time then reads what he or she "really" did this summer. The humorous combinations are sidesplitting.

—Glenn Davis, Winston-Salem, North Carolina

HALLOWEEN CAROLS

If you're puzzled about how to celebrate Halloween in a way that's both fun and honors the Lord, perhaps you should try a "Halloween Caroling Party."

Here are a couple songs for you to try:

WE ARE YOUR TRICK-OR-TREATERS
(Sung to the tune of "Rudolph, the Red-Nosed Reindeer")

We are your trick-or-treaters
And we have a song or two
We aren't here for the candy
This time we just came for you.

Hope you don't mind the singing
We don't want to make a scene
We came because we wanted
To wish you happy Halloween.

BETTER WATCH OUT
(Sung to the tune of "Santa Claus Is Coming to Town")

Oh, you better watch out
And don't go outside
The things we have seen
Make us horrified
Don't you know it's Halloween night.

There's bogies and bears
Werewolves that bite
Scary things that go
Bump in the night
Don't you know it's Halloween night.

They see you through the darkness
Like bats in deep, dark caves
It's not you that they hunger for
It's candy that they crave.

(Repeat first verse.)

Several of our young people filled goodie bags with cookies and special sweets for four or five elderly folks from our church. On Halloween evening all the youth came in costumes to the church and we left together for this event. The elderly people were visited, presented with the goodie bags and serenaded by the youth with these Halloween carols. We had devotions at the last house and then returned to the church for refreshments, games and a costume contest.

Our hosts really enjoyed the songs and the special visits and our kids were thanked for months afterward.

—Durand Robinson, Birmingham, Alabama

HALLOWEEN TREAT NIGHT

On Halloween night, our group gives out treats and friendship for the older and shut-in people of our community. We call it "Halloween Treat Night."

We ask people in the congregation to bring candy and baked goods to the church the Sunday before Halloween. We compile a list of people in our church and community who might benefit from a friendly visit on Halloween night. Then, on Halloween, we canvass the area, visiting people, singing to them and leaving goodies. A party back at church finishes off a fun Halloween.

We began this enjoyable project about 15 years ago. Our visitation list grows a little each year. The older people seem to like the visits; some of them keep a watch for us.

An interesting variation for "Halloween Treat Night" might be to distribute food and clothes to needy families.

—Katherine Smithberger, Lower Salem, Ohio

JIGSAW JACK-O-LANTERNS

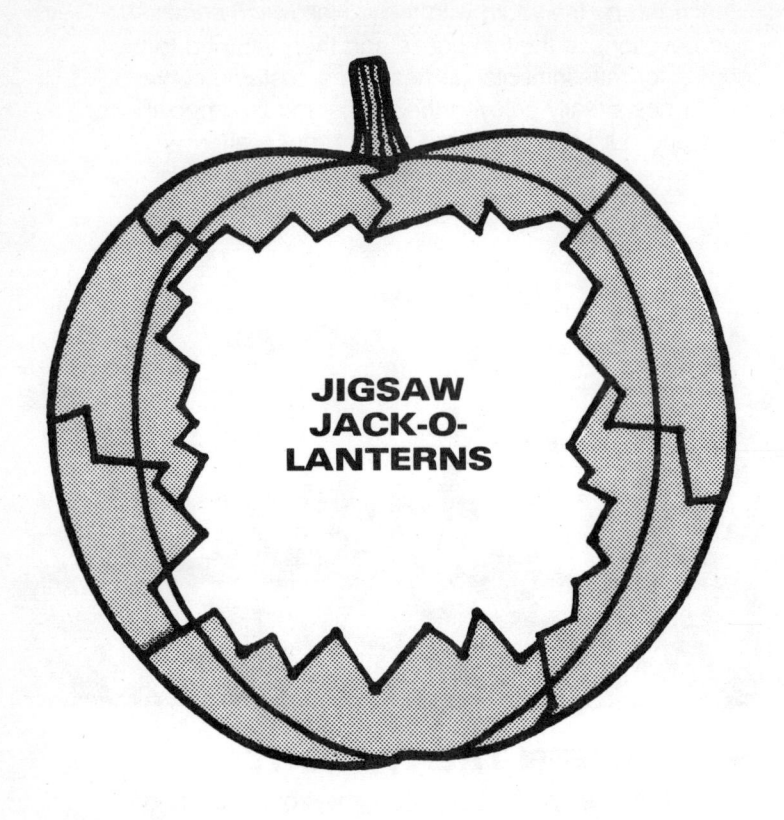

This is a great competitive team sport for Halloween.

Give each team (two or three persons per team) a pumpkin and a sharp knife. Then give each team only one minute to cut up the pumpkin into no more than 10 pieces.

Then have the teams rotate to a different pumpkin. Have a supply of round wooden toothpicks. Give each team two minutes to put its "jigsaw puzzle" pumpkin back together, using the toothpicks to hold the pieces in place.

The first team done or the team with the most "together" pumpkin after the time limit is the winner. Pumpkins must be able to stand up alone to be considered a winner.

—Dan Scholten, Rhinelander, Wisconsin

THE SPOOKY STORY

Here's an idea for your next Halloween lock-in or other late-night scary time.

Divide the group into the following sound effects: **Night sounds**—Adult leaders pick a vegetable name and softly repeat its name. **Wind**—Three or four people softly whistle. **Thunder**—Each person claps hands once, in succession. Begin on the right side of the room and flow to the left. **Rain**—In unison, everyone snaps his or her fingers quickly, then rubs palms together rapidly, then pats thighs and finally claps hands rapidly. Soften the "rain" by reversing these actions. **Howling**—Three or four people howl like coyotes. **Footsteps**—Three or four people slowly say, "schlop, schlop, schlop." **Scream**—All girls scream at high pitch. **Moan**—All guys give a long, low moan.

After rehearsing the sounds, someone with a deep, clear voice reads the spooky story. The sounds come in when the cue word is read.

"It was a dark, cold night. The full moon was bright, its light pierced gray, menacing clouds. The light cast strange shadows through the woods and across narrow, grassy fields. **Night sounds** echoed through the darkness. (Pause.) **Wind** whispered through the pines, singing its song so softly. Suddenly, the **wind** increased in intensity, shaking the leaves and branches back and forth, back and forth. A great clap of **thunder** broke through the night as a jagged lightning bolt lit up the sky. It began to **rain.** (Pause.) The **rain** beat down on the dried leaves and began to fall harder and harder. Soon the ground became a damp, gooey mud. In the distance the **howling** of dogs was heard through the **wind** and **rain.** The sound of **footsteps** was heard moving slowly through the thick mud. All at once another **thunderclap** broke through the night and a piercing **scream** rose above the trees. As the **rain** began to soften and the **wind** died down, a low **moaning** could be heard through the forest. Suddenly, all became silent. (Pause.) And nothing could be heard (pause) except for the **wind.**"

—Ben Sharpton, Gainesville, Florida

CHRISTMAS BEDTIME STORIES

Being a kid again can be lots of fun—especially when everyone else is being one! Use this idea to give your group members a special treat this holiday season.

Invite your young people to bring their favorite stuffed animals and meet in your home one evening after church. Have them sit around the Christmas tree. Light some candles and dim the lights.

Now, read a thought-provoking Christmas story or legend. Have volunteers tell about Christmases they remember most. Add a short devotion, prayer and Christmas carols. Close your time together with home-made cookies and hot chocolate.

This idea worked well with our group. Everyone brought a stuffed animal and thoroughly enjoyed the evening, reminiscent of childhood bedtime stories with mom, dad and good ol' teddy.

—Shari Pendleton, Indianapolis, Indiana

CHRISTMAS CRAFT TIME

Help your young people work on Christmas gifts, have a good time and get to know each other better!

Find out which of your young people like to work on crafts and arrange for an evening when you and interested group members can get together. Work on Christmas craft projects; your group members may want to work on individual gifts or prefer to work together on a big project. They may want to work at different crafts or prefer to make the same craft. Be flexible. Offer special instruction in crafts if your young people would like to learn new skills or if they need help with their project(s). Group members or adults in your church may be able to teach crafts.

Last year the girls in my group met together and learned how to quilt. They all worked on separate projects; some made pillows and some made wall hangings. Everyone had a great time.

—Karen Musitano, Benton, Pennsylvania

CHRISTMAS WAFERS SALE

If you're searching for an interesting fund raiser that helps the poor and needy during Christmas, try selling Christmas wafers. We have raised as much as $800 in one weekend.

Christmas wafers are a Polish/Slavic tradition. These wafers are shared among family members before the evening meal on Christmas Eve. They are made of thin, unleavened bread and measure about 6 inches by 4 inches. Everyone is given a wafer (a pink wafer is given to the youngest). A family member then wishes another member a "Merry Christmas" and other blessings. The well-wisher then breaks off a piece of the other person's wafer and eats it. The other family member then reciprocates the act.

Our group sells the wafers during Advent. We advertise the sale through fliers and articles in the church bulletin. We sell packages of four wafers (three white, one pink). The packages sell for 50 cents or a larger donation. Christian supply stores may be able to supply you with wafers. You can order the wafers directly from Christmas Wafers Bakery, P.O. Box 99, Lewiston, NY 14092. Its phone number is 716-754-7198. The bakery offers the wafers, envelopes to sell them in and instructions for use in family worship.

Our sales have been very profitable. We make it clear that the profits go toward helping needy people during the holiday season. Christmas wafers are a beautiful way of sharing the holiday with the family, the church and the community.

—Paul Lippard, Sterling Heights, Michigan

COLOSSAL CHRISTMAS CARDS

For a song-filled surprise, have your group send giant singing Christmas cards.

As a group, design a large, colorful "Christmas card" from two sides of a refrigerator box. Cut and fold the box to create a card-like effect. Use bright tempera paints or wrapping paper to add pictures and words on the front. On the inside, cut numerous holes for people's heads. They stand behind the card, stick their heads through the holes and sing the special Christmas message.

Pile your group and the colossal card in the back of a van or pickup and drive to the first home. Have one person greet the recipient and explain that your youth group is delivering a unique Christmas card. Open the card. With everyone behind the card, heads through the holes, sing and share the joyful message of Christ's birth. Continue to the other homes.

Christmas cards and caroling will never be the same!

CRAZY CAROLS

Caroling parties are as much a part of the holiday season as crowded stores, fruitcake and mistletoe. Why not spice up the caroling party concept this season? All you need are inexpensive musical instruments: kazoos, Humanatones, slide whistles, party horns, spoons, saucepan covers, cowbells, etc. You'll also need a crazy, fun-loving group of backup singers.

Use "Crazy Carols" to entertain and surprise inactive youth group members, shut-ins, the little kids in Sunday school, even busy shoppers in the malls. Chances are your carolers will make a years-long impression on those who hear you.

> we wish you a merry christmas stop.
> we wish you a merry christmas stop.
> we wish you a merry christmas stop.
> and a happy new year stop.

SINGING CAROL-A-GRAMS

This idea is a great Christmas-time fund raiser/service project/fun time. We sold "Singing Carol-a-Grams" to people in the church.

We took orders for three weeks. Our order form included a space where carol-a-gram senders could write a message. Christmas cards could also be provided for the messages. The carol-a-gram senders also wrote down a carol they wanted us to sing to the receivers.

On the carol-a-gram delivery day, we split into two groups and went from house to house, sang a carol, wished them a "Merry Christmas" and delivered the sender's yuletide message.

We delivered 60 carol-a-grams, mostly to the church's shut-ins. The people genuinely enjoyed both sending and receiving carol-a-grams.

—William D. Wolfe, Lansing, Michigan

GROUP GROWTH GOODIES

BUILD A BODY

This crowdbreaker is a nice introduction to a session on the body of Christ or Christian unity.

As each group member arrives, give him or her a piece of paper on which is written the name of a body part (head, arm, leg, foot, appendix, heart, etc.). When you give the signal, everyone must locate all the others with the same body part. When a group is complete, it should shout out its name.

Then instruct group members to scatter and form complete bodies. The first one to form should shout, "We're number one!" For more competition, have the completed bodies race to cut large body parts from construction paper and create giant people.

—Larry J. Michael, Rockville, Maryland

CANDLELIGHT FRIENDSHIP

This activity helps build friendship and unity in a group. It works well with mature teenagers in a retreat or evening setting.

Have everyone sit in a circle on the floor. Light a candle and turn off the lights. Give the candle to someone to hold; each person should say something nice about the candle-holder. Then the candle moves to the next person in the circle and the process continues. Make sure everyone has a turn holding the candle.

—John W. Herron, Phoenix, Arizona

DESIGNER JEANS

Here's a fun way to use today's fashions to lift up our appreciation for others' unique gifts.

Draw a large jean pocket on an 8½x11 piece of paper. Each young person receives a photocopy of a pocket and is told to write his or her name on the label and then describe, on the pocket, the kind of person that would wear these jeans (emphasizing what the wearer does or feels). Example: Mary Jones Jeans. The kind of person who wears Mary Jones Jeans likes summer more than winter, has long talks with old friends and watches the sunrise alone.

Afterward, each person shares his or her designer jeans description. The leader notes that all have identified themselves in a positive way. Read Psalm 139 (especially verse 14) and thank God for the "wonder of you."

—Dan McGill, Montevideo, Minnesota

FRIENDS DURING THE WEEK

This creative communication aid works during the week rather than at the youth meeting itself.

At a meeting, distribute 3x5 cards and ask each person to write his or her name and telephone number. Notice which group members aren't present and also fill out cards for them.

Put all cards in a basket and have each member pick one. Deliver cards to members who aren't present and "fill them in" on what's happening.

Challenge your young people to be special friends during the week to the person whose name they picked. They could send notes of encouragement and appreciation; they could telephone their person to see if there are any prayer needs; they could leave little friendship packages—cookies, messages, etc.—in his or her school locker; the possibilities are unlimited.

Group members will get to know each other better. And as more friendships are developed outside of the church environment, your group will realize a stronger unity when all members are together.

—Michael Yengo, Iselin, New Jersey

GROUP BIRTHDAY PARTY

After a lot of labor by many people, our youth group was finally born. We chose to throw a birthday party to celebrate our new beginning.

Our party had all the trimmings—birthday cupcakes, balloons, party plates, party cups, party napkins, lots of games and other fun stuff.

Near the end of the party, we shared a short ceremony of dedication to the group. Each person was given a birthday cupcake (one small candle per cupcake). One at a time, each member expressed a wish or hope for the new group. After all had shared, we lit the candles. In unison, "So let it be done" was voiced and the candles were extinguished.

We've decided to make the birthday party an annual celebration. It helps us remember where we've been, how we've grown and where we're going.

—Judy Lindhag, Almira, Washington

LIGHT IN THE DARKNESS

Here's a bright idea for a rainy day.

Arrive at your group's meeting room early and set a candle in a place where it can be seen but not easily noticed. Light the candle.

When group members arrive, read together John 1:6-13 and discuss possible reasons why people didn't pay attention to Jesus. Have the group list the ideas.

After a few minutes of the discussing and listing, quietly turn off the lights. Then encourage group members to think why they didn't realize the candle was in the room. Compare their thoughts with the ideas on the list.

Close your discussion with the challenge of Matthew 5:16.

—Scott Welch, Nicholasville, Kentucky

LOVE LETTERS

To give your group members a special sense of love and belonging, use this idea for your next retreat.

Before the retreat, ask group members' parents to secretly write love letters to their sons and daughters and give the letters to you or other group sponsors. Be sure to contact all the parents and to collect letters from all the parents; you wouldn't want anyone to be left out.

At the retreat, find the right moment—perhaps after a study on family or love—and present the letters to your young people. Give them the freedom to be alone to read their letters.

My group did this and not only were the group members treated to a special dose of love, the parents said they noticed changed attitudes in their kids when they returned.

—Barb Silcox, Norwalk, Ohio

MEATLESS DINNER

Instead of the standard staples for youth group dinners,(e.g., pizza, burgers or hot dogs), why not organize a meatless dinner? A week before the dinner, divide into two- or three-person teams. Each team is responsible for preparing a nutritious meatless casserole for the next week's youth dinner. Bring recipes to the dinner, too.

The meatless dinner can be a great setting for discussions on hunger and simpler lifestyles. It can also be a part of a fund raiser for your denominational hunger programs.

—Margaret Shauers, Great Bend, Kansas

NEWCOMERS' NIGHT

Many senior high youth groups welcome incoming freshmen with a special event at the start of school in the fall. Why not welcome them into your group at the end of the school year before, so they can join the group in summer activities?

Our group welcomed newcomers with a special dinner in their honor. We sent each graduating junior higher a personal invitation to join the senior high group members for dinner at a local restaurant. We met together at the church first. Senior highers paid for the newcomers' meals.

If you have a large group, ask for individual group members or group officers to volunteer to sponsor new members for the dinner rather than having the whole group attend.

Use the welcoming dinner as an opportunity to distribute your summer calendar and highlight upcoming events.

Our dinner helped incoming members feel accepted and more comfortable with the senior highers.

—Barry Barrios, Pearland, Texas

POSTER DAY

"Your group ought to be in pictures," someone told our group. So, we got into a BIG picture: a poster. We called all members, inactives, boyfriends, girlfriends, put an ad in the church newsletter, searched the highways, byways and arcades. We shouted it from the mountain, tree and table tops that "Poster Day" was coming.

A member in our church took several snapshots of our "mob." We sent one of the photos to a company that enlarges photographs into full-size posters. (Ads for these companies can be found in several magazines such as Seventeen.)

We hung the posters in our meeting room, gave them as gifts and even sold a few. "Poster Day" went over so well that we plan to make it an annual event.

—Bryan Carter, Cynthiana, Kentucky

PUZZLE UNITY

To illustrate a retreat on the theme of group unity, I purchased a poster and cut it into puzzle pieces (one for each member, plus five extra pieces). On the bottom of the poster I wrote "Let's get it together . . . now."

I placed each piece in an envelope and sealed it. On the outside I wrote, "Bring to retreat." The envelopes were given or sent to each retreat-bound member. I kept the five extra pieces.

At the retreat, each person opened his or her envelope and all tried to put the picture together. Of course, some of the pieces were missing. This led to a discussion about how each piece contributes to the whole picture, about each member's responsibility to the group and our unity in Christ.

We covered the puzzle with clear contact paper and hung it in our youth room at church as a reminder that the picture is not complete without each person contributing to the whole.

—John Ward, Pontiac, Michigan

SENSE SCRIPTURES

Here's an idea to help the Bible touch the senses as well as the intellect. It's a good way to begin Bible study, discussions and informal gatherings.

First, the selection from the Bible is read aloud. Then, all close their eyes. The passage is read aloud again. They are to use their imaginations to sense the biblical story, try to set themselves in the middle of the story and then tell what they see, hear, smell, taste and feel.

Start with a sense-pounding Bible story such as Jesus calming the sea in Mark 4:35-41. Responses in our group were:

SEE—darkness; big, black clouds; lightning; huge waves.

HEAR—thunder; splashing; men screaming; boat creaking.

SMELL—rain; salt; wet people who didn't smell good anyway.

TASTE—water; salt; cottonmouth caused by fear; lunch coming up.

FEEL—seasick; the boat rocking; humidity; fear; anger (because Jesus was sleeping); confusion; helplessness.

This process sets the mood for digging into the meaning of the text. The Bible is easier to understand if you can imagine yourself in the middle of it.

—John Collins, Houston, Texas

SHOPPING MALL ADVENTURES

For a good time and good learnings, take your group to a shopping mall for an afternoon or evening.

Send out group members for the first 45 minutes to shop and enjoy each other's company, but also to observe "commercialism" as it appears on products and advertisements. Then meet together at a central point to discuss what we're "supposed" to be like according to these ads or products (for example: tall, thin, attractive)—and what God says we should be like (for example: loving, kind, patient).

The next 45 minutes is to study shoppers—how they act, what their attitudes are, etc. Then meet and compare some generally accepted attitudes toward life (for example: getting) and what Jesus said and how he lived (for example: giving).

Finally, scatter to observe sales clerks. Meet at an ice cream shop this last time and discuss how the clerks seem to see their roles—as servants or bossy-type people? Do they act like they're doing a favor when they offer help, or like they really want to help? Together think about servanthood as Christians and look at examples from Jesus' life.

—Mark C. Bigley, San Antonio, Texas

TAPE RECORDER PARABLES

Try this simple idea: Choose a parable and think of the sounds that accompany it. Then tape record the parable—with the sound effects, of course.

The methods are varied: (1) Create a recording for presenting to group members during a study of a particular passage. (2) Let small groups of members choose different parables and spend 45 minutes working on recordings for presenting to the whole youth group.
(3) Have all group members work together to produce sound effects and record a parable for presenting to the congregation.

Whatever the method, imagination is important. If your passage says, "And when he comes home," record the stomp-stomp-stomping of footsteps and the sounds of opening and closing a door. Improvise. If the passage talks about sheep, record a chorus of the young people "b-a-a-ing."

And when your "work" is done, sit back, relax and listen—really listen—to the Bible passages.

TINKERTOY TEAMS

Have some fun with tower building—and group building at the same time.

First, prepare by taking several large sets of Tinkertoys, dividing each set in half, and packaging each "half" in a large plastic bag. You'll need one bag of Tinkertoys for every six people in your group.

Now, split members into groups of six and give each group a bag of toys. Instruct them: "This exercise takes 10 minutes. For the first five minutes, examine the toys in your bag without removing them from the bag. Then discuss your ideas, and on paper design the tallest, strongest tower you can build with the toys. Then you will take five minutes to construct your tower—but you can't speak to each other during its construction. You may communicate in other ways, but not by talking."

When the 10 minutes is up, call time and give each group a copy of these questions to discuss: Did you build what you designed? How did it feel to work together? What did it feel like to be a member of your team? Were you supportive of each other?

Gather all members together in one large group and ask members of each small group to explain what their tower "means" and what they discovered about themselves as they worked on building it.

—Glenn Davis, Winston-Salem, North Carolina

WE ARE THE BODY

Here's an original idea for scripture reading and a way to have total audience participation in its interpretation.

Split your group into four sections. Each is assigned a letter of the word "PART" and each section is designated as a hand, foot, eye or ear.

You'll also need a reader, sign holders, Bible, two large posters ("The body is one" written on one poster and "We are . . ." written on the other) and four smaller posters with the letters P-A-R-T.

The reader begins with 1 Corinthians 12:12-26. Whenever the word "body" is read, the reader pauses, the sign holder raises the sign "The body is one" and everyone shouts the poster message with his or her right fist raised. The reader continues in this manner; every time a "part" is read, the reader pauses, the sign holders raise the letter signs, and the four sections shout the letters P-A-R-T cheerleader style! When "eye" is read, the sign holder raises the "We are . . ." sign and the eye section yells, "We are the eye" as they blink their eyes. (Ear section tugs on their ears, hand section waves and foot section stomps three times.)

This activity provides the body of Christ with involvement and participation in this scripture reading and has been well received every time we've used it.

—David Hatfield, Mount Vernon, Illinois

used 3-8-81

WHAT'S IMPORTANT?

This exercise helps to decide what's really important in life. Everyone receives five 3x5 cards.

Write the five most important things in your life on the cards (one item per card). These can be objects, persons, desires, goods, relationships, abilities, whatever. The leader then asks the following questions:

1. Do any of your cards concern objects such as money or clothes or a car, etc.? It has been stolen . . . drop these cards to the floor.

2. Do any of your cards concern relationships with a person of the opposite sex (boyfriend or girlfriend)? That person has just dropped you . . . drop these cards.

3. Do your remaining cards refer to your special talents or abilities (athletics, music, etc.)? You've suffered a terrible accident and can no longer use those talents . . . drop these cards.

4. Do your remaining cards have something to do with relatives such as your parents? They've suddenly died . . . drop these cards.

5. Keep any cards you have not dropped. Don't pick up any cards already dropped. Discuss these questions: What cards are in your hand? Could you live with only that? What card was most difficult to drop? How would you feel if you actually lost what you wrote on the cards?

6. Finally, study Matthew 6:33—"Seek first his kingdom and his righteousness and all these things shall be yours as well."

Matt. 6: 19-34 —Glenn Davis, Pfafftown, North Carolina

"WHO'S HIS" NEWS

Boost youth group morale, get more visibility and help church members get better acquainted with group members: Run a regular "Who's His" section in the church newsletter or bulletin.

Send parents "student profile" sheets that ask for basic information about their young people: grade, school, activities, interests, honors and awards, etc. I also asked for confidential information about how the parents view their young people's spiritual lives.

Prepare a "Who's His" logo to help people recognize

this new, regular section.

Feature one or two group members per newsletter or bulletin. Let the "who" be a surprise.

My group loves this! They get to know each other better, and the ones in the limelight really get a lift (and wonder where I got all that information).

—Jeff Boyd, Austin, Texas

YOU ARE THERE

We got this Bible study idea from the old **You Are There** television show.

We choose a topic for Bible study, then we pick a place to study.

"You Are There" Bible studies are easy to imagine: Go to a cemetery and conduct a study on death; lock up the group in a jail to study Paul's imprisonment; go to a hilltop and make an altar for Abraham's near-sacrifice of Isaac; Lamentations in a deserted, crumbling church building; outdoor surroundings for Psalm 23; Jesus' birth in a barn or cave; a desolate area for Jesus' temptation in the wilderness; study some of Jesus' healing miracles in a hospital chapel, then split up and visit some of your congregation's ill people; find an absolutely dark place for a light/darkness study of 1 John; study the Revelation to John on an island. Skimming through the Bible releases all kinds of study ideas.

Let curiosity and excitement build for "You Are There" Bible studies by keeping the topic and place of the study a secret.

We've found that "being there" helps our Bible studies come alive. And, it's a fun way to learn.

—Garry Baldwin, Burlington, North Carolina

YOUTH BREAKFAST WEEK

Each spring our church holds "Youth Breakfast Week." About 500 junior and senior highers from our county meet weekdays before school from 6:30 to 8 for breakfast and to listen to an inspirational Christian speaker or musician. Sponsored by our county youth council and city ministerial association, the breakfast brings churches of all backgrounds to work together.

Here's how we do it: The program is handled by the associate pastor of our church, since the event is held there. He begins booking speakers and musicians in September and wraps it up before Christmas. After the new year, a theme is developed and the speakers and musicians are informed.

Our church youth group takes care of publicity.

A woman in our church recruits other churches to assist in planning breakfast menus and orders the food. Each morning volunteers from a different church prepare breakfast.

The churches involved in this event raise money to cover expenses for the food, speakers and musicians.

Transportation to local junior and senior high schools is provided following the event each morning. City churches donate the use of their buses.

"Youth Breakfast Week" has been so well received it has been held every spring for over a dozen years now. Our community appreciates its effective method of communicating to youth that people care about them.

—Douglas L. Suggs, Asheboro, North Carolina

FUN
FUND
RAISERS

BOX 'EM UP

If your church is near a college or university, this fund raiser is for you.

Every year, at break time and the closing of classes for the summer, students face the problem of finding packing boxes, packing and studying for finals. Your group can sell boxes on campus as a service to the students and the youth fund. Here's what to do:

Contact the college or university; talk with the director of residential life and find out the school's break times. Explain your idea and ask for permission to sell boxes on campus.

Then get to work. Contact local businesses and ask them to save boxes for you. Some grocery stores save boxes for the general public, so you'll want to make periodic pickups. You'll need a storage area (someone's garage works fine) to keep and sort the boxes according to size.

Three weeks before the break, go to the campus and get permission to hang posters which advertise your service. You could also send fliers about your sale to dorm residents through the on-campus mail service.

Arrange to have the use of a truck—or two trucks if you have lots of boxes. Make a big sign to call attention to your box sale; charge 25 cents for medium-size boxes and 50 cents for large boxes.

Sale day should be about two weeks before the school's break. Go to a dorm parking lot and set up your big sign by the truck. Set sample boxes next to the sign. You'll need someone to collect boxes from inside the truck for your customers, someone to collect money, and others to help tote boxes to the dorms when bulk purchases are made.

And if your group is really ambitious, why not set up a lemonade stand, too?

—Kari B. Fisher, Pueblo, Colorado

CHILI-MAKING FUN

This activity is sure to warm up the wintertime and add spice to any youth group.

Have a chili-making contest and fund raiser! Challenge your group members and other church members to compete against each other in pursuit of the best tasting chili.

Publicize the contest/fund raiser well in advance. Generate excitement and interest. Have competitors fill out entry forms and state how much chili they will make. Also have purchasers place orders which specify how much chili they plan to buy. Make sure you will have enough; plan on more than you have orders for.

Hold the contest/sale on a Saturday afternoon in the church or in a member's home.

First, the contest: Ask your pastor and a few other church officers to be the judges. Line up samples of the entries in numbered bowls. Provide glasses of water, spoons, bibs and voting cards. When the judges make their selection, award your winner with a large chili bowl, scoop and a bottle of mouthwash.

Then, the sale: Fill small, medium, and large containers with the chili and determine prices for the different amounts. Sell away!

This can be lots of fun. Try it!

—John Miller, Shavertown, Pennsylvania

CHRISTMAS CRAFTS FAIR

Our youth groups help Christmas shoppers avoid the mad rush by sponsoring an annual "Christmas Crafts Fair" at our church. The fair has grown into a great congregation-oriented activity.

We invite artists from our congregation and the area to participate in the fair, held the first or second weekend in December. Each artist/craftsman pays $25 to rent a booth. We provide a table, chairs and coffee and doughnuts during the morning set-up time.

Publicity is absolutely essential. One month before the fair, the group plasters the community and schools with posters, fliers and news releases to the media and other churches.

The night before the fair, the groups decorate and set up booths in a corner of the church's parking lot. (Churches in colder climates will need to sponsor the fair indoors.)

In the morning, the youth help the artists get their displays ready. Some of the members don clown outfits and Santa suits, entertaining the crowds and giving candy canes to children. Some of the members baby-sit the kids inside the church, letting the little ones color and create crafts while their parents shop for arts and crafts outside. We also sell coffee and doughnuts.

The artists/craftsmen usually sell lots of their products. The shoppers genuinely enjoy the friendly atmosphere, quality handmade gifts and helping out the group.

Our expenses are about $50. Twenty-five artists usually rent space. We clear about $575. We should make even more this coming Christmas when we expand to 30 artists and provide a hot dog stand for noon shoppers.

—Marie Paneno, Los Angeles, California

DOUGHNUT DELIVERIES

Our youth group delivers doughnuts on weekends as a service to the church and community—and our youth budget. Here's how we do it:

The youth take orders for freshly baked doughnuts from their families, friends, neighbors, etc. We charge $2.65 per dozen, which includes delivery between 8 and 9 on Saturday morning. A baker in town gets up early to make the doughnuts (you may have an all-night doughnut shop where you could buy them.) One youth picks up the doughnuts and takes them to the church where the rest of the youth collect them for delivery to the homes. We profit 70 cents per dozen doughnuts.

—Beverly Perry, New Albany, Indiana

FIREPLACE STARTERS

Fireplace owners will appreciate this: Your group can make and sell attractive fireplace firestarters.

You'll need: a paper cutter, kitchen tongs, cardboard boxes, shoe boxes, scrap cloths, ribbons, markers, scissors, glue, tape, 9x9 old baking pans, half-or-more-burned candles, an outside grill, charcoal, lighter fluid and matches. Put a notice in your church newsletter and bulletin to solicit items you need.

When all is ready, find a spot on someone's patio or back yard and set up shop. One person should use the paper cutter and cut the cardboard boxes into 4-inch squares. Another person should tend the grill and, as necessary, put candles into the baking pans to produce the wax. The next person should use the kitchen tongs to dip the cardboard squares into the heated wax and then set the wax-coated squares on cardboard (not yet cut) for drying. Some group members should decorate the shoe boxes with the scrap cloth pieces, ribbons and markers. And finally, others should count 50 cooled firestarters and neatly pack them into each decorated shoe box.

Working right along, your group can produce 400 to 600 fireplace firestarters an hour. It takes a bit longer to finish attractively packaging them.

A box of 50 for $1 looks like a real buy. Depending

on the amount of tinder and kindling in a fireplace, it takes only one or two firestarters to get a great fire going. They ignite with a single match and burn completely, leaving no wax residue in the fireplaces.

Choose a cold church morning and sell your firestarters after the worship service; business will never be better.

—Len Aalberts, Iowa City, Iowa

FRUIT KABOBS SALE

Bake sales are great fund raisers. People seem to enjoy them—except for weight watchers. So, we held a "Fruit Kabob Sale" as an alternative to brownies and cake. We bought a watermelon, three honeydew melons, two pineapples and a few mangoes.

Before our Sunday evening service, we gathered in the church kitchen. Some cut the fruit into chunks and others speared a chunk of each fruit onto wooden fondue sticks. We made about 90 of these fruit treats, laid them on trays and put them into the refrigerator. Following the benediction, we pulled the trays out of the refrigerator. We served the kabobs with punch and coffee.

Weight watchers weren't the only ones who appreciated the kabobs. Even the heavy eaters liked the variety of fresh fruit. We made about $40 in donations within 30 minutes.

—Don Warner, Rosemead, California

GREAT PUMPKIN AND APPLE FESTIVAL

Each year on the Sunday before Halloween, our youth group sponsors a "Great Pumpkin and Apple Festival." The preparations for this are as much fun as the sale itself.

On the first weekend in October, the youth and adult advisers drive to an apple farm and spend an afternoon picking up six to eight bushels of apples. Most varieties of apples are ripe then, so there is a large selection. You can probably buy apples from a market at a reasonable price, but we think picking them is more fun.

During the next two weeks, we polish and sort the apples. We distribute some to church members who have volunteered to bake cakes, pies, doughnuts or breads (all containing apples). We bag some for sale, and we keep out about 200 which we use to make caramel apples a couple days before the sale.

Finally, we purchase about 250 various size pumpkins from a local farmer and set them outside the church. We set up tables of the baked goods, bags of apples, caramel apples, cider, coffee, etc., and sell the goods after the worship services and to the community. Apple products are usually sold out; leftover pumpkins are donated to a child care center.

We profit about $300.

—Cynthia Malow, Sterling Heights, Michigan

GUTTING BUILDINGS

Your group can earn lots of money by gutting old houses and buildings.

Banks are always foreclosing or buying old houses needing repair and renovation. Contractors often shy away from gutting buildings. They are far more interested in buying buildings that are ready for plumbers, electricians and carpenters to begin work immediately.

First, meet with bank officials. Explain that your group is interested in providing a community-oriented service to earn funds. The group will provide the tools, safety gear (hard hats, safety goggles, etc.), insurance and experienced adult supervision. The bank will pay the group for the service, the sum depending on the going rate for gutting buildings.

Undertake a small house as your first project. You'll love ripping out old paint-covered wallboard, wood lath, ceilings and windows. Arrange to have pickups or dump trucks haul the debris to the nearest dump.

Depending on the dimensions of the building, your group can earn hundreds of dollars for one or two days of work. You'll learn helpful skills, provide a useful service to your community and have lots of fun.

—Paul E. Housworth, Flushing, New York

HAUNTED MAZE

This unforgettable activity is a variation of the maze idea printed in **The Youth Group How-to Book** (see page 80). Halloween will never be the same again after you hold this fund raiser at your church.

Build a maze by connecting several large appliance boxes. Each maze section should lead to a haunted room. We had a safari room complete with cavemen and wild animals; a spook haven featuring Frankenstein, ghosts and goblins; and a Dr. Jekyll operating room. (A youth group member sat inside a box with only his head poking through the top. His head looked as if it were detached from his body and sitting on top of the operating table.)

We charged 75 cents admission for people to crawl through our haunted maze—if they dared—and all proceeds went to a world hunger program. Our church was proud of our youth group when they found out that the $122 collected from this fund raiser went to a worthy cause.

—Mark T. Ludwick, East Berlin, Pennsylvania

HELP-A-THON

The "Help-a-Thon" helped us raise some cash and become aware of the needs in our community. We took a Saturday in the fall to work on the homes and yards of the elderly and handicapped in our community. We helped them ready their homes for the cold months ahead.

For each hour of work, we raised pledges from friends at school, family and church members. Most people were eager to support our effort to help the elderly and handicapped.

Working for the people gave us a deep sense of satisfaction; most were so happy to have someone simply talk with them. And, we got a lot of important work done. It was an experience we will remember for a long time.

—Dave Jones, Bloomington, Minnesota

HELP THEM GIVE

Here's a fund raiser that provides a needed service to rest home residents.

Check with the rest home ahead of time to get permission to hold a Christmas gift bazaar. Get any special guidelines or suggestions. Also find out when is the best time to visit and if it's okay to hang posters announcing your bazaar.

Gather the gifts: Request donations from church families. Make some craft items. Create Christmas decorations and cards; be creative. Have a variety of gifts and cards to offer.

Take your group and its wares to the rest home. Enjoy the visit! Talk with the residents and share the spirit of Christmas with them.

Keep prices low enough to be affordable and offer tag-writing and gift-wrapping services. Also provide free delivery of gifts to local families.

Remember to sing Christmas carols to the residents before you deliver the gifts.

—Margaret Shauers, Great Bend, Kansas

MISSION MARATHON

Marathons often bring in big bucks but too often fail to accomplish anything of real significance. So, we sponsored a "Mission Marathon."

Members found sponsors for every hour spent at the marathon (24 hours). A variety of worthwhile projects and learning activities focused on missions. During the marathon, speakers from various youth missionary movements came to share their organizations' goals and ministries. Films were shown on missionary efforts in hungry lands, the inner cities and our own life situations.

Most important, we worked on several projects to help missionaries. We packaged bars of soap for missionaries. (Little bars of used soap were given to us free from hotels. Soap is greatly appreciated at many mission stations.) For medical missionaries we rolled bandages from strips of used bed sheets. Hotels and congregation members donated the sheets. And, we canvassed the neighborhood for cans and packages of food.

We raised $2,200 for the group from pledges, mailed l,400 bars of soap to missionaries, shipped 700 8-foot bandages to medical missionaries and collected 684 cans and packages of food for local food banks. And, we received a nice write-up in the local newspaper (a great morale booster).

—Greg Chantler, Tacoma Washington

1950s DRIVE-IN

Our church parking lot turned into a **Happy Days** scene one spring for our "H&K's Drive-In" fund raiser. Named after pastors Howard Vanderwell and Kenneth Schepel, "H&K's Drive-In" raised more than $500 and was a fantastic experience for the group.

A large menu posted on the building offered hamburgers, hot dogs, french fries, coffee, soda pop and ice cream. Bubble-gum-chewing, roller-skating carhops took orders and skated trays of food to customers. All of the food was prepared on gas grills at a large work area facing the cars. Everyone dressed in the '50s theme: leather jackets, bobby socks and greased hair. The customers seemed to enjoy watching the members work and laugh together. Free pieces of bubble gum came with each order. Music from the '50s blared into the parking lot.

Our drive-in was open from 5 to 7:30 p.m. on a Saturday. In that time we served 400 hamburgers and 150 hot dogs.

Our expenses: hamburgers, hot dogs, french fries, cooking oil, coffee, soda pop, ketchup, mustard, relish, onions, bubble gum, napkins, order pads, pens, paper cups for ice cream, plastic spoons and skate rental. Several of these items were donated by fast-food restaurants and several stores gave us church discounts. A local baker let us use white aprons for the cooking crew and a lumber dealer gave us nail aprons for the carhops to keep change. Six gas grills were loaned to us by church members.

We publicized the drive-in with posters, fliers and press releases. A local newspaper featured us with a nice report and photos.

We earned a good profit, had a lot of fun and relived the nostalgic days of the '50s era drive-ins.

—Kenneth Schepel, Hudsonville, Michigan

PENNIES MAKE SENSE

A contest was the sensible approach for a fund raiser in our church. We pitted the men against the women in a race to collect and contribute the most pennies for the youth fund.

We set up a large, old-fashioned wooden scale with copper buckets in the church lobby. The men were to load one bucket with pennies; the women, the other. The contest lasted eight weeks, and each Sunday the youth would empty the buckets, count the pennies and prepare the next week's bulletin insert, which announced the accumulated results and also kept up interest and enthusiasm.

Some people wanted to contribute but did not have pennies, so we accepted silver and bills but would then exchange those at a bank. We wanted pennies so that, following the contest, we could line them up side by side and try to win a spot in the **Guinness Book of World Records.**

The youth group spent an evening wrapping the pennies. The fun part was taking the wrapped coins to the bank—in exchange for $400.

—Matt Fabry, Las Vegas, Nevada

PENNY SATURDAY

Thinking "big" is ambitious, but sometimes thinking "small" is more beneficial—it was for us in this fund raiser, anyway. Our youth group asked church families to part with their jars or boxes of pennies and spare change. We explained our goal was to get enough coins to be able to form a mile-long chain.

We announced well ahead of time that on a certain Saturday we would lay all the donated change on the church parking lot. Thanks to a good promotion crew, that Saturday the coins came rolling in.

The sun-baked coins lined up one by one made quite a spectacular sight and many people stayed to watch. By the end of the day we had laid down $700 worth of coins, mostly pennies!

—Tom Franks, Hayward, California

TIN CAN FORTUNE

This project will serve your community and raise funds for your youth group. We think it's a lot of fun, too.

Get pledges for each discarded can or bottle you can collect. Then when the big day arrives, give group members trash bags and send them out in pairs to hit the roadsides, parks, schoolyards and any other places such litter might be found. You might also go door-to-door requesting cans or bottles.

Have kids meet back at the church or someone's house at an appointed time to sort the cans and bottles, tally the amount of money raised and tell about their adventures. You might want to award your first-place garbage-collecting team with a free pass to the city dump or some other appropriate token. Don't foget to drop off the goods at recycling centers.

Do this project on a Saturday and report back to your church members the next day—and start collecting the real goods!

—Alan Kieffaber, Dayton, Ohio

NOTE

Have you participated in a fun, original youth group activity? GROUP Magazine is on the lookout for creative, unique youth group games, parties, retreats, discussions, special events, worship ideas and fund raisers.

If your group has an idea, submit it to the following address:

"Try This One"
GROUP Magazine
P.O. Box 481
Loveland, CO 80539

You will receive a check for every idea we publish.

OTHER YOUTH MINISTRY RESOURCES FROM
Group Books

COUNSELING TEENAGERS, BY DR. G. KEITH OLSON. The authoritative, complete and practical reference for understanding and helping today's adolescents. Hardbound, 528 pages. $19.95.

THE BASIC ENCYCLOPEDIA FOR YOUTH MINISTRY, BY DENNIS BENSON AND BILL WOLFE. Answers, ideas, encouragement, and inspiration for 230 youth ministry questions and problems. A handy reference. Hardbound. $15.95.

THE GROUP RETREAT BOOK, BY ARLO REICHTER. This is *the* resource for start-to-finish retreat planning, execution and evaluation ... plus 34 ready-to-use retreat outlines. 400 pages. $15.95.

HARD TIMES CATALOG FOR YOUTH MINISTRY, BY MARILYN AND DENNIS BENSON. Hundreds of low-cost and no-cost ideas for programs, projects, meetings and activities. $14.95.

THE YOUTH GROUP HOW-TO BOOK. Detailed instructions and models for 66 practical projects and programs to help you build a better group. $14.95.

THE YOUTH GROUP MEETING GUIDE, BY RICHARD W. BIMLER. This resource provides years of inspiration, ideas and programs for the most common youth group activity—the meeting. $11.95.

CLOWN MINISTRY, BY FLOYD SHAFFER AND PENNE SEWALL. Everything you need to know to begin a clown ministry or enhance your present ministry. Includes 30 detailed skits and more than 50 short clowning ideas. $7.95.

YEARBOOK: UNTOLD STORIES, BY BILL WOLFE AND JANITA WOLFE. Each page of this book shares experiences from the viewpoint of a person looking back on his or her high school years. The readers will examine their struggles and feelings in their search for self-identity, friends, acceptance and God. $5.95.

LEADERS GUIDE FOR YEARBOOK: UNTOLD STORIES, BY BILL AND MARTHA WOLFE. This leaders guide is a *must* for youth group use of **Yearbook: Untold Stories**. More than 70 meeting outlines, a retreat outline and a large-group event outline. $6.95.

THE BEST OF TRY THIS ONE (Volume 1). A fun collection of games, crowdbreakers and programs from GROUP Magazine's "Try This One" section. $5.95.

MORE ... TRY THIS ONE (Volume 2). A bonanza of youth group ideas—crowdbreakers, stunts, games, discussions and fund raisers. $5.95.

TRY THIS ONE ... TOO (Volume 3). Scores of creative youth ministry ideas. $5.95.

STARTING A YOUTH MINISTRY, BY DR. LARRY KEEFAUVER. An insightful book with tips on starting a youth ministry program or revitalizing an existing program. $5.95.

FRIEND TO FRIEND, BY J. DAVID STONE AND LARRY KEEFAUVER. Provides a simple yet powerful method for helping a friend sort through thoughts, feelings and behaviors of life problems. $4.95.

Available at Christian bookstores or directly from the publisher: Group Books, P.O. Box 481, Loveland, CO 80539. Enclose $2 for postage and handling with each order from the publisher.